For Grégoire, Aubin, and Octave, my own shower of roses.
S. B.

Original French edition:
Thérèse de l'Enfant-Jésus
© 2009 by Mame, Paris
© 2011 by Ignatius Press, San Francisco • Magnificat USA LLC, New York

ISBN Ignatius Press 978-1-58617-622-8
ISBN Magnificat 978-1-936260-15-7

The trademark MAGNIFICAT depicted in this publication is used under license from and is the exclusive property
of Magnificat Central Service Team, Inc., A Ministry to Catholic Women, and may not be used without its written consent.

Printed by Tien Wah Press, Malaysia
Printed on February 8, 2011
Job Number MGN 11002

The Life of a Saint

Thérèse
The Little Flower of Lisieux

Text: Sioux Berger – Illustrations: Elvine

Translated by Janet Chevrier

Ignatius

MAGNIFICAT®

The Little Flower

Have you ever heard about the town of Lisieux? Thousands of people go there on pilgrimage every year. It was in this town in Normandy, France, that Saint Thérèse of the Child Jesus, known as the Little Flower, grew up. Today, Thérèse is known the world over. Yet, before becoming a great saint, she was a little girl just like any other.

Here is her story . . .

Thérèse was a very happy little girl. She lived in Alençon with her parents and her four big sisters, Marie, Pauline, Léonie, and Céline.

One day, she found her mother lying in bed, looking very pale.

"Mama, aren't you well?" exclaimed Thérèse with surprise.

"No, my little one, I'm not very well. You are going to have to be very brave. I'm very ill and am going to go to heaven."

Thérèse's mother looked tenderly at her daughter and sighed. Thérèse was only four years old, but she understood that her family would soon be stricken by a great sorrow . . .

When their mother died, Thérèse and Céline were still very little.

What was to become of them? They so needed comforting! So Céline threw herself into the arms of her sister Marie and cried:

"Well then, you will be my mama!"

And Thérèse, who always did everything just like Céline, said:

"Well then, Pauline will be *my* mama!"

Left alone with five daughters, Thérèse's father worried about their education. He agreed to move to Lisieux, where his wife's brother lived with his family. He found a house there surrounded by a big garden.

"The house is called 'Les Buissonnets'",* he explained to Thérèse. "You'll see, my little queen, we'll be happy here."

"Oh, yes, Papa! Look how beautiful the garden flowers are!"

Thérèse's father smiled. A simple drop of water on a rose petal, and she was delighted!

Yet, since the death of her mother, Thérèse often cried. She found comfort in talking to Jesus. She would then feel the sun dawning in her heart.

One day, Pauline found her hiding behind her bed curtains.

"What are you doing there?" she asked her. "Are you hiding?"

"I was thinking", answered Thérèse.

"But thinking about what?"

"I was thinking about the good Lord, about life, about eternity . . ."

Secretly, Thérèse was already dreaming of giving her life to Jesus.

*The French word for "little bushes"

The days passed so quickly at Les Buissonnets! When Thérèse was ten, Pauline decided to enter Carmel* to become a nun.

"I want to go, too!" Thérèse said to her.

"You're too young!" replied her sister. "In the meantime, you can come and visit me."

Thérèse burst into sobs. She had already lost her mama, and now here was Pauline about to leave her as well! She was so unhappy she fell gravely ill. She seemed to lose her senses. She did not recognize anyone anymore. The doctor was very worried.

"Let's pray", Marie suggested to her sisters. "The Blessed Virgin will console us." And they knelt down before the big statue of the Virgin Mary near Thérèse's bed.

And on the day of Pentecost, a miracle happened: Thérèse smiled and began to speak again!

That evening, Marie plied Thérèse with questions:

"Thérèse, tell me what happened!"

"The Blessed Virgin was so beautiful," answered Thérèse, "more beautiful than anything I've ever seen before. Her face radiated such indescribable goodness and tenderness; but what went right to the depths of my soul was her ravishing smile."

*Carmel refers to a Carmelite convent

Thérèse kept the Virgin's smile deep in her heart. On the day of her First Communion, she was so moved, she wept for joy.

Two years later, on Christmas, Thérèse felt the power of God within her, and this certainty made her stronger: she cried much less often and became very brave.

From then on, she knew what she wanted to be when she grew up: she would be a saint! She wanted to be a Carmelite, for she was now sure that prayer could work miracles!

One day, she asked Céline to have a Mass said for her intentions.

"And for whom do you wish a Mass to be said, my Thérèse?" her sister asked kindly.

"Well . . ." said Thérèse, "it's for a criminal condemned to the guillotine. He refuses to see a priest before dying. His name is Pranzini. Oh, if only my prayer could save his soul!"

That evening, Thérèse prayed very hard for Pranzini. The day after his execution, she opened the newspaper. What she read there made her melt in tears: just before dying, the criminal had asked to kiss the cross of Christ!

"So Jesus heard me!" thought Thérèse.

The years went by. Marie joined Pauline in Carmel. Thérèse was almost fifteen. She, too, wanted to give her life to Jesus, and she went to her father to make her request:

"Papa, I would like to enter Carmel. I can't wait anymore."

"You're very young, my little queen. The bishop and the superior of the Carmelites will refuse."

"But, Papa, I want to go! I want to love Jesus and make him loved. I can only do that by entering Carmel. I must go right away. I'll go ask the Holy Father's permission if I have to!"

Thérèse sobbed. Deeply moved, her father clasped her in his arms.

"Ah!" he sighed, "the good Lord does me great honor in asking me for my children like this . . ."

Then he picked a little white flower and gave it to his daughter.

"You see, Thérèse, God gave life to this pretty flower and took care of it day after day."

"Jesus will protect me just like this little flower", thought Thérèse. And she is still known today as the Little Flower of Lisieux.

So many obstacles were put in Thérèse's way! Everyone refused to let her enter Carmel. Her father decided to go to Rome with Thérèse and Céline.

After weeks of pilgrimage, Thérèse was finally able to see Pope Leo XIII. "Remember, it is forbidden to speak to the Holy Father", explained the priest who accompanied them.

But Thérèse disobeyed. She could not stop herself from speaking. She knelt before the Holy Father, placed her hands on his knees, looked him right in the eyes, and exclaimed:

"Most Holy Father, permit me to enter Carmel at the age of fifteen! If you said yes, everyone would be happy to agree!"

Astonished, the Pope leaned toward the little girl, blessed her, and replied:

"Come, my child, you will enter Carmel if the good Lord wills it!"

Thérèse wept with emotion, but two guards were already escorting her out of the reception hall.

The Pope had not said yes, but Thérèse remained confident. On the day before her birthday, she finally received a letter from the bishop: it was all settled! Everyone had given his consent. At last, she was going to be able to enter Carmel in the footsteps of her sisters Pauline and Marie!

In Carmel

"I'm going to be able to pray for priests and sinners!" Thérèse told herself as she entered Carmel on April 9, 1888. On seeing the cell where she was to live, Thérèse was full of contentment. How small it was! A bed, a stool, a little jug . . .

"I'm here forever", she repeated to herself with joy. Soon, she would be called Sister Thérèse of the Child Jesus.

The rules of convent life were harsh. The day started at five o'clock in the morning, followed by housework, laundry, dishes, and sewing. There was no heating, and there were six hours of prayer a day.

Hardest of all, Thérèse was not allowed to speak to her sisters Pauline and Marie, even though they were so close. In Carmel, you cannot chat whenever you like!

And then, you had to learn to live with the other sisters.

There was one who particularly annoyed Thérèse. The things she said and did got on her nerves. But Thérèse understood that to love others is the path that leads straight to Jesus. So she made a decision:

"I'm going to treat this sister the way I would treat the person I love the most!"

And when that sister asked her why she was being so kind to her, Thérèse replied:

"It's because I'm happy to see you, of course!"

Thérèse did not tell her that it was Jesus she saw, hidden in the depths of her heart . . .

Thérèse tried not to complain and to be good-humored with all the sisters.

She made many little efforts to be a saint, but it was not easy. Compared to the great saints of history, she felt like a tiny grain of sand. The road before her seemed long, and holiness, like a huge stairway of steep steps.

She wanted to go more quickly to Jesus. For that, the ideal would be . . . an elevator, that new machine that had just been invented!

"I would like to find an elevator to raise me up to Jesus," she said to herself, "because I'm too little to climb the rough stairway of perfection."

And yet, she did not give up.

One day, during prayer, she read these words of God: *Whoever is a little one, let him come to me! . . . As a mother caresses her child, so will I comfort you.* "How tender these words are!" thought Thérèse. "I have nothing to fear, then. I just need to stay little! It is your arms, O Jesus, that will be the elevator to lead me to God!"

But little by little, Thérèse began to wonder if she had really chosen the right path. She was very happy in Carmel, but was this really where God wanted her to be? In her prayers, she did not seem to hear any answer to her questions. She sometimes even fell asleep in the chapel!

During recreation, the sisters talked about missionaries, priests who traveled to Asia, to Africa . . . about sisters who left to found Carmels abroad.

How wonderful, Thérèse dreamed, to carry the word of Jesus to the ends of the earth. She wanted to be everything at the same time: saint, Carmelite, wife, mother, apostle, priest, doctor, martyr, missionary! But it would take more than one life to do it all!

In prayer, Thérèse realized that what all these lives have in common is the Love of Jesus. Then everything seemed to become clear. What did it matter if one were in Carmel or on the other side of the world? What mattered was to love.

"My vocation is Love!" she rejoiced. "I've found my place. In the heart of the Church, my Mother, I will be Love . . . that way, I will be everything . . ."

Thérèse liked to write poems and plays and to draw pictures.
She was an artist!

Her sister Pauline, who had become superior of the convent, asked her to write her memoirs.

Thérèse obeyed, and, in the evenings in her cell, she wrote in a little school notebook what would become *Story of a Soul.*

Yet, Thérèse was tired; she was ill. She was suffering from tuberculosis. In those days, there was no cure for this illness.

But Thérèse kept her sense of humor and could make the whole community laugh. One was never bored with her!

"The health of Sister Thérèse is getting worse", one of the sisters recounted. "She suffers very much but makes fun of herself: she says her cough is as loud as a steam engine!"

A Shower of Roses

Thérèse grew weaker and weaker. Whenever anyone asked her how she was, she always answered:

"I'm fine! You mustn't be sad if the Lord calls me to heaven . . . I feel that it is in heaven that my mission is going to begin, my mission to make the good Lord loved as I love him! After my death, I will let fall a shower of roses upon the earth!"

She sensed that, after her death, she would send upon the world a shower of graces—gifts from God to mankind.

Thérèse could no longer leave her bed, and the sisters took turns at her bedside. She suffered greatly but continued smiling.

Death did not frighten her. She reassured the sisters:

"I will be of more use in heaven than I am here. I want to spend my heaven doing good on earth. No one who invokes me will ever go unanswered."

One evening, as she lay dying, Thérèse gave a long look at the statue of the Blessed Virgin, pressed her crucifix to her heart, and, with her last breath, murmured:

"Oh, I love him! My God, I love you!"

Then her face became peaceful, and her suffering seemed over. The sisters prayed together beside her. Thérèse went to heaven with a wonderful smile on her lips.

One of the sisters, stricken with an incurable illness, wept at the foot of her bed. When she raised her head, she sensed she could walk on her own: she was cured!

Just as Thérèse had so desired, a shower of roses had begun to fall. Through her intercession, miracles happened.

$\mathcal{N}$ews of Thérèse's death spread throughout Lisieux.

A year later, her memoirs were published. People began to read them. They came in great numbers to Lisieux on pilgrimage. They prayed to Thérèse, invoked her, and were heard!

$\mathcal{I}$n 1908, a little girl of four and a half fell ill and went blind. Her name was Reine,* and medicine could not cure her.

On the advice of a nun, her mother decided to take her to Lisieux.

$\mathcal{W}$hen they arrived at Thérèse's graveside, they began to pray very hard. All of a sudden, Reine shouted:

"Mama, I can see! Mama, I see!"

"Oh, my God! My daughter is cured! It's a miracle!"

*The French word for "queen"

News of the miracles spread quickly. The sisters received up to four hundred letters a day! They kept these anonymous testimonies very carefully until, a few years later, they were published in a seven-volume collection. Entitled *The Shower of Roses*, it recounts all the miracles that occurred after the death of Thérèse.

People came to Lisieux by the thousands, the crowds growing larger day by day. There was an endless stream of carriages from the train station! In people's hearts, Thérèse was already a saint . . .

Thérèse was canonized in 1925. Pope Pius XI laid a golden rose on her tomb as a sign of veneration.

Today, missions on every continent bear her name. In 1927, the Pope declared her patroness of the missions, like Saint Francis Xavier, the great Jesuit who had traveled to China!

Thérèse's book has been read by millions of people. It was in 1997 that Pope John Paul II proclaimed her a Doctor of the Church to make it known that what she had written is a true teaching about Love.

And so it was that Thérèse's dreams came true.

Feast Days

The feast day of Saint Thérèse of the Child Jesus and of the Holy Face is October 1.
Thérèse died on September 30, 1897, and is still commemorated every year in Lisieux on the Sunday closest to this anniversary.

Thérèse, patroness of the missions

Thérèse said: "I would like to proclaim the Gospel on all five continents of the earth,
even to the most remote isles . . ."
In Carmel, her prioress asked her to write letters to the missionary priests whom she supported with her prayers.
Thérèse had wished to "travel over the whole earth". For over ten years now,
Thérèse's relics have toured the world, and thousands of pilgrims come to see them and pray.

The little way

Saint Thérèse strove to put love into everything she did.
Her "little way" was to remain humble and to seek to come close to God by making little efforts in everyday life.
She said: "I want to find the means of going to heaven by a little way that is very straight, very short, and completely new."

Thérèse, Doctor of the Church

It is due in part to her wonderful discovery of this "little way" that Thérèse was declared a Doctor of the Church.
This means she was so close to God that she was able to know him well and to help us love him better.
So, we can read everything she said and wrote as a true teaching about God.

Thérèse's parents

Zélie and Louis Martin were declared blessed by the Pope on October 19, 2008.
This means they are recognized as heroes of the Church, having worked day after day to live according to the Gospel
and to raise their children in the love of God and of others.

Thérèse's brothers and sisters

Thérèse was the youngest of a family of nine children, four of whom died young. Her four elder sisters all became nuns.
Marie, her godmother, Pauline, and Céline entered the Carmel in Lisieux,
like Thérèse. Léonie entered the Visitation convent in Caen.

Carmel

The Carmelite Order is a very old religious order founded by hermits who lived near Mount Carmel in the Holy Land,
following the example of the prophet Elijah. The order was reformed in the sixteenth century by two Spaniards,
Saint Teresa of Ávila and Saint John of the Cross. The Carmel in Lisieux was founded in 1838.
When Thérèse entered in 1888, there were twenty-six sisters.

The town of Lisieux

Today in Lisieux, you can still visit the various sites that played a part in the life of Saint Thérèse
—Les Buissonnets, the cathedral, the Carmelite chapel, which houses her shrine—
as well as the huge basilica built to receive the many pilgrims who visit each year.